The Boom Years

The foot of Lonsdale Avenue, North Vancouver's business and transportation center, photographed from one of the North Vancouver Ferry and Power
Company's ships, circa 1908. Virtually every man-made feature visible in this
view did not exist before 1901.

The Boom Years

G.G. Nye's Photographs of North Vancouver

1905 - 1909

Written and compiled by

Donald J. Bourdon
North Shore Museum and Archives

Hancock House Publishers
North Vancouver, 1981

Copyright © 1981 North Shore Museum and Archives
ISBN 0-88839-117-X

Canadian Cataloguing in Publication Data

Nye, G.G. (George Gordon), 1885-1958.
   The Boom Years

   Bibliography: p.
   ISBN 0-88839-117-X

   1. North Vancouver (B.C.) — Description — Views.
   I. Bourdon, Donald J. II. Title.
FC3849.N67N9   917.11'33   C81-091199-X   F1089.5.N67N9

Editor Margaret Campbell
Design/Production Peter Burakoff
Layout Diana Lytwyn and Linda Rourke
Typeset by Sandra Sawchuk in Garamond type on an AM Varityper Comp/Edit
Printed in Canada by Friesen Printers

Cover: Published by J.V. Valentine and Sons, this post card of the Hotel North Vancouver was produced from a G.G. Nye photograph taken in approximately 1907.

Credits: The illustrations in this publication are reproduced with the written permission of the following sources:
   Photographs—North Shore Museum and Archives
   Map-North Vancouver City Public Library
   Cover post card-Arthur Davies, private collection

   Photographs reproduced for publication from original negatives and vintage prints by Don Bourdon and Ken Smith

Published in Canada by

HANCOCK HOUSE PUBLISHERS
#10 Orwell Street
North Vancouver, B.C., Canada
V7J 3K1
Tel. (604) 980-4113

Contents

To Margie

Preface

"For Fine Photographs, go to G.G. Nye, The Pioneer Photographer." So recommended an advertisement of 1908,[1] and during the few years that George Nye was in business, North Vancouverites did just that. The fine photographs which have survived from Nye's commercial enterprise document the growth of a British Columbia town propelled by the swell of nationwide expansion at the turn of the century. This publication's intent is to pay tribute to the "Pioneer Photographer," who photographed North Vancouver with skill and enthusiasm for a short but formative period of its history.

The Boom Years is also intended to stimulate interest in today's visible links with North Vancouver's roots. These include what remains of the urban landscapes created during the community's infancy and the natural beauties which attracted residents to the North Shore throughout the Edwardian era. By publishing a selection of Nye's photographs, the North Shore Museum and Archives hopes to illuminate North Vancouver's "boom years." At the same time, we hope to awaken concern for the vanishing buildings and landscapes that George Nye and his contemporaries enjoyed and admired.

In 1970, after resting for years in an attic, the extant photographs of G.G. Nye were donated to the new North Shore Museum and Archives to form the nucleus of its photographic holdings. The Archives Sub-Committee first discussed the idea of an exhibition of Nye's work during August of 1975. Over the next four years, an exhibit entitled "The Boom Years: A Portrait of North Vancouver by G.G. Nye, Photographer, 1905-1910" was slowly assembled. A selection of reproductions was finally opened to the public in the summer of 1979. *The Boom Years* is based upon that exhibit, with additional photographs and a revised text.

Without the donation of the Nye photographs to the North Shore Museum and Archives by the photographer's daughters, *The Boom Years* would not have been possible. Many people aided with the process of combining what I consider the best of Nye's photographs with an explanatory text to produce this publication. I wish to thank the staff of the North Shore Museum and Archives for their asssistance with this long-distance project. The British Columbia Heritage Trust was most generous in agreeing to aid this undertaking when the Museum and Archives first contemplated producing a book. Their contribution is greatly appreciated.

My special thanks to the following friends for their help, information, and advice: Bill Baker, Ed Cavell, Margie McDougall, Bernice McLean, Molly Nye, Ken Smith, Henry Tabbers, June Thompson, Irene Tucker, and Smitty Waugh.

George Nye's photographs have given me hours of pleasure and through them I have gained an appreciation for his life and times. I hope that this work will give the same kind of enjoyment to its readers.

D.J. BOURDON
Calgary

9

Introduction

At the turn of the century, North Vancouver was little more than a series of black lines printed on a townsite map. A dozen years later it had evolved into an incorporated city possessing all the material amenities available. This transformation was typical of the remarkable growth taking place throughout the nation during a boom that was based upon widespread prosperity and a confident national self-image. Canadians had good reason to feel confident during these years. The boom time had come for a country that offered free land on its plains to the immigrant and plentiful natural resources to the investor. The addition, in 1905, of Alberta and Saskatchewan to confederation and the astounding settlement phenomenon on the prairies confirmed the belief that indeed the twentieth century belonged to Canada. These years were not without instances of "financial stringency" but, for the most part, the nation enjoyed unprecedented growth from the late 1890s until 1913.[2]

North Vancouver's dramatic rise during these years was due primarily to a population surge in adjacent Vancouver and to the appearance of distinct suburban districts on that port city's perimeter. Between 1901 and 1911, Vancouver's population more than tripled to over 100,000 residents. Correspondingly, the population of North Vancouver soared from 365 in 1901 to more than 8,000 ten years later.[3] The city's progress could be demonstrated by citing concrete facts and figures. However, the boosters' optimism was also based upon anticipated expansion and promised services. Some schemes proposed for North Vancouver at this time, including a railway link with the North and a bridge across the Second Narrows of Burrard Inlet, only took tangible form years later. George Nye focused his view camera on the physical manifestations of this optimism. The resulting photographs show a landscape changing daily because of the momentum of city building at that time.

By 1900, photography had reached a stage where it could be mastered by both the professional and amateur practitioner. The professional photographer found markets where special expertise was necessary or where multiple copies were required. These markets included portraiture, architectural and industrial photography, souvenir views and post cards. Many photographers catered to the "postal" fad that was popular throughout the Edwardian world. Post cards were used not only as a method of communicating short messages, but also as a means of exchanging collectible images. Canadians sent approximately 27,000 post cards in 1900, 41 million in 1908, and more than 60 million during 1913.[4] Both black and white photographic and color lithographic cards were in fashion. Monochrome photographs were often enhanced by lithographers to create colorful mass-produced "postals." Post cards showed Canada to the world with photographic accuracy. As a producer of both color and monochrome post card views, George Nye shared a common role with many of his small-town colleagues who were actively documenting their communities for the same purpose.

Despite obvious limitations, George Nye's photographs tell us much about North Vancouver from 1905 through 1909. The community appears a paradox: a modern city imposed upon a timeless forest. With the sudden construction of roads and buildings, this longstanding natural wilderness was receding. Yet the forces that propelled these conspicuous changes were erratic. The underlying economic momentum was to collapse and rally in succession in the years to follow.

A substantial urban landscape is visible in the photographs reproduced here, suggesting that the participants were not pioneers in the sense that their contemporaries scattered thinly over the prairies were. But North Vancouverites were hardly urban dwellers even by 1905 standards. The industrial development and social disparity visible in larger and older centers was less developed in North Vancouver.

When examining Nye's photographs today, one could easily assume that the boom years were prosperous, peaceful, and even carefree. Perhaps in many ways they were. However, signs of turbulence are also present in these images, despite Nye's intention to idealize his subjects. Man's impact on the environment is apparent in some views, and the pressures of a new Anglo population upon the native population is implied by others. For their ability to please and provoke, the "pioneer photographer's" works serve as valuable records and visual treasures.

George Gordon Nye, North Vancouver's first professional photographer, was born in February, 1885 into a large family in Brighton, England. His parents, A.D. (Arthur) and Catherine Nye, joined the throngs of English travelers bound for Canada following the CPR's completion, and in 1890, they settled at the transcontinental's terminus, Vancouver. An economic depression in the mid-1890s restrained real estate activity in North Vancouver, but in 1898, when land values were rising and property sales resuming, A.D. Nye purchased one acre of property from the North Vancouver Land and Improvement Company.

The Nyes were one of only a handful of families residing in North Vancouver when they built their home at Sixth Street and Chesterfield Avenue. During 1901, in return for Boer War military service, two of George's brothers were each granted a quarter section of land, one in Lynn Valley, the other in North Lonsdale. Another brother pre-empted land in Lynn Valley so that on the eve of the land boom which swept British Columbia, the Nyes held a considerable amount of property in North Vancouver. In addition to participating in the residential development of North Vancouver, the Nyes were active in the affairs of the municipality. George's brother, Thomas S. Nye, served as a District councillor, and their father as a magistrate.[5]

About 1905, at the age of twenty, George Nye opened his photographic business near Lonsdale Avenue and the waterfront. The services and products he offered included "picture framing, portraits and landscapes, copying and enlarging, local views, amateur supplies, souvenir cards and blueprints...."[6] Nye submitted black and white views to the British firm, J.V. Valentine and Sons, which had offices in major Canadian cities. Examples of color post cards survive, indicating that his customers could choose from colored "postals" or the photographically printed cards processed in Nye's studio.

In 1908, Nye married. The September 18 *Express* announced that:

> ...on Saturday last... George Gordon Nye, a well known business man of this city, was united in the bonds of holy matrimony with Bertha M. Janes, likewise of this city.... Mr. and Mrs. Nye will reside on 2nd Street, where cozy apartments have been arranged in connection with the photographic studio operated by Mr. Nye.

Examination of existing photographs indicates that Nye pursued his career as a photographer most actively before his marriage. As the Nyes began to raise a family, George considered an alternative occupation. About 1910, near the height of the building boom, he discontinued professional photography and turned to the more lucrative carpentry trade, which he followed until his retirement. George Nye died in 1958, after having witnessed remarkable changes in North Vancouver over sixty years.

G.G. Nye on Grouse Mountain, 1906.

Photographs

by George Gordon Nye

The Boom Begins....

Nye's Photo Studio
George G. Nye is the pioneer
photographer of North Vancouver, and his
new and up-to-date studio is located on
Second street, half a block off Lonsdale
Avenue. He does good work, many of the
views in this issue being his handiwork. He
has recently added another branch to his
business, that of picture framing. A fine
collection of local views and souvenir post
cards are always kept to choose from. Mr.
Nye is well and favorably known, having
been a resident here for a number of years.

The *Express,* Christmas Number, December 1, 1906

By the turn of the century, prosperity was
returning to the nation, and this sparked the
beginning of North Vancouver's development. In
the first dozen years after 1900, the area enjoyed a
period of land speculation and residential
expansion, accompanied by civic and commercial
growth. On the strength of an upturn in the world
economy, several large land concerns, which had
acquired substantial properties during the depressed
1890s, opened their tracts for residential sale. To
keep pace with the optimism and influx of settlers,
the municipality built roads and initiated modern
services. In 1907, the City of North Vancouver was
incorporated, encompassing the townsite area of the
District.[7]

A new urban landscape began to appear amidst
the fire-scarred forest on the North Shore foothills.
This community rapidly eclipsed waning Moodyville
to the east and the Indian mission settlement to the
west. A business district grew up in Lower Lonsdale,
the junction of a transportation network comprising
the British Columbia Electric Railway Company's
streetcar system and the North Vancouver Ferry
and Power Company's ships. The latter company's
ferries linked the North Shore with the sprawling
city across the harbor. Proximity to the Inlet also
placed North Vancouver in a favorable position
with respect to coastal trade.

The years 1905 through 1909, during which
Nye was in business, coincided with a period of
intense optimism that peaked prior to the First
World War. Like other Canadians, North
Vancouverites were inspired by the prospect of
prosperity. Their confidence in the future was
inflated by the land sale boom and anticipated
railway development. When viewing Nye's
photographs today, one can gain a sense of the
aspirations of North Vancouver's builders, their
attitudes toward homes, parks, industry, local
government, and private enterprise. These images
convey the social climate prevailing in a community
and a country unaware of impending social upheaval
and world war.

Mr. and Mrs. A.D. Nye and their children, circa 1895. George, the youngest, is seated on the floor. Photographer unknown.

George's mother, Catherine Nye, in the parlor of their Sixth Street home, circa 1905. Family portraits by Nye are visible throughout the room.

This view shows Second Street West from its intersection with Lonsdale Avenue. Nye's studio is the small building on the left in the distance.

Lonsdale Avenue, from the Ferry Wharf, circa 1905. The street railway, sidewalks, electricity, and telephone services had yet to come.

LONSDALE AVE
FROM WHARF
NORTH VANCOUVER

When viewed from the same spot one year later, the Lower Lonsdale area had changed. Utilities had been installed, and municipal and commercial activity was thriving.

LONSDALE AVE NORTH VAN. BC

Lonsdale Avenue and First Street East, circa 1907. Here a small crowd listens to a band concert on the lawns of the City Hall. The decorations suggest that it is a holiday.

Dominion Day excursionists at the Ferry Wharf, circa 1908. A visit to the North Shore from Vancouver involved several transfers—from streetcar to ferry and back to tram at the base of Lonsdale Avenue.

The British Columbia Electric Railway Company's line handled freight as well as passengers, though not too successfully at times. While transporting electric motors to a saw mill, this engine slipped, sending a passenger car hurtling into Burrard Inlet. Circa 1907.

The S.S. *Lonsdale* was the first ocean-going steamship to dock in the new city. It discharged its cargo destined for the Klondike at Cates Wharf in September, 1909.

$\mathfrak{C}$ity fathers and guests at City Hall, Dominion Day, 1907.

On July 1, 1907, the City of North Vancouver celebrated its recent incorporation. The official designation of a city distinct from the rest of the municipality had been accomplished over the previous two years through the efforts of a group of businessmen, capitalists, residents, and politicians. Their occupations and interests are indicative of some of the forces active in the decade preceding the First World War. Pictured in this portrait of the city fathers are many of the key personalities in North Vancouver's property boom.

W.J. Irwin, a realtor, was one of the participants in the City's incorporation. Thirty years after Nye photographed North Vancouver's founders, Irwin described the gentlemen who posed for the photographer on Dominion Day, 1907:

Sitting left to right

1. Hon. F. Carter-Cotton, member of the Legislative Assembly of B.C. for several terms. Provincial Minister of Finance. (Now passed to a higher sphere of activity.)
2. J.C. Keith, Esq., a distinguished pioneer citizen, Owner of extensive land holdings in the Province. Keith Road and the Keith Block in North Vancouver were named after him. (Now passed).
3. Arnold E. Kealy, Esq., Reeve of the District of North Vancouver and first Mayor of the newly incorporated City. Now a resident of Los Angeles. Served several terms as Reeve, Councillor and Mayor.
4. Edward Mahon, Esq., President of the City of North Vancouver Land and Improvement Company Ltd., which then owned large tracts of land in North Vancouver, and subsequently donated the Grand Boulevard area after they had borne the expense of clearing same. Also conveyed Mahon Park to City, in Perpetuity, at one-half of its estimated value. Mr. Mahon was the sixth son of Sir William Vesey Ross Mahon, Bart., and Lady Mahon, of Castlegar, County Galway, Ireland. (Now passed—in June 1937, age 75.)
5. Alderman W.H. May, former Reeve of District North Vancouver, and subsequently Mayor of the City of North Vancouver for several terms. One of the early Pioneers of the Province.

Standing right to left

1. Hon. Macpherson, for many years Postmaster of the City of Vancouver, and subsequently Member of Parliament for the Vancouver Riding. (Now passed.)
2. Alderman W.J. Irwin. Served as Councillor of District of North Vancouver prior to City's incorporation, some ten terms as Alderman in the City, and one term as Mayor. Was organizer and first Secretary of the North Vancouver Board of Trade (in 1906) and subsequently President.
3. J.J. Woods, Esq., for many years Assessor for the District and City of North Vancouver. Several terms Director of the North Vancouver Horticultural Society.

4. Ex-Mayor Garden of the City of Vancouver. Served several terms on the Council and in other public capacities.
5. Alderman William F. Emery. Served several terms on North Vancouver City Council.
6. Alderman Alexander Smith. Served several terms on the City Council, also as Chairman of the Public Hospital Committee. Was President of the North Vancouver Board of Trade for one term. (Now passed.)
7. Reeve Byrne, of the Municipality of Burnaby, a guest of the North Vancouver City Council. (Now passed.)
8. Mayor Alexander Bethune of the City of Vancouver. An invited guest on the occasion of joint celebration of "Dominion Day" and Incorporation.
9. Alderman D.G. Dick. Served several terms as Alderman. Was President of Board of Trade. The Principal organizer and first Master of the first Masonic Lodge in North Vancouver following incorporation of the City. There had been a Lodge in Old Moodyville when the mill was operating there. (Mount Herman.)
10. Police Chief Arthur Davies. Many years of public service.
11. Alderman Alfred Crickmay. Several terms on Council.
12. Mr. Robb, a Reporter for many years with the World Newspaper. (Passed.)
13. Alderman A. McKay Jordan. Several terms. A distinguished Scientist. (Passed.)
14. Alderman W.J. Dick. For many years a Member of the City Council. (Now passed.)

The above memo was made by me on July 1st, 1937, on the thirtieth anniversary of the City's incorporation.

(Signed) William J. Irwin [8]

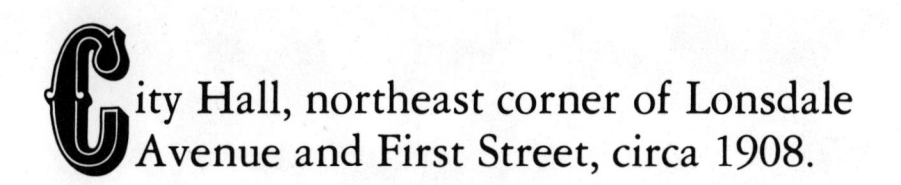

City Hall, northeast corner of Lonsdale Avenue and First Street, circa 1908.

Albert Nye's residence was situated on the northeast corner of Fourth Street and Chesterfield Avenue. As it appeared shortly after construction, circa 1906.

A buoyant economy made it possible for people of both wealth and modest means to realize their residential ambitions in North Vancouver. The financial climate facilitated the construction of fine homes, expressions of prosperity. It also enabled those of lower incomes to build bungalows and clear gardens. Residences ranged from elaborate architect-designed homes situated on Lonsdale Avenue, to one-room shacks surrounded by forest. Big or small, these homes fulfilled a widespread desire for privacy and independence, aspirations symbolized by the single-family dwelling.

The Civic Committee urged all to "Build your home in North Vancouver" where the following conditions could be enjoyed:

Unexcelled advantages as a residential center, choice homesites, unobstructed view, moderate prices, no taxes on improvements, purest water direct from mountain springs, best natural drainage, sewage system about to be installed, excellent roads and conveniently located hotels throughout the district, water works, electric light, electric cars, unexcelled social, educational, religious advantages, unequalled scenic attractions on north, east or west within few miles, the delight of tourists, many ideal nooks for picnic parties, half hourly ferry service to and from Vancouver.[9]

Although the Committee's description was excessive, North Vancouver did have much to attract the prospective home owner.

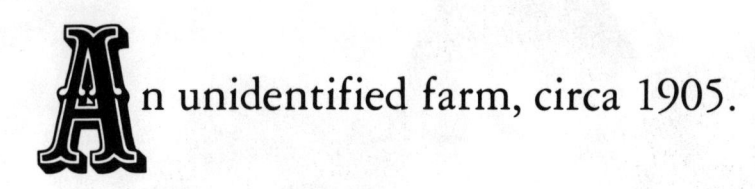

An unidentified farm, circa 1905.

William J. Irwin's home, situated north of Fourth Street on Lonsdale Avenue. Irwin, a realtor, served as Mayor and Alderman of the City. His home was demolished in 1975.

This view, from "the bend" in Lonsdale
Avenue at Eighth Street, shows the
residential landscape in 1906. The home in the
foreground belonged to J. Burnes, a carpenter. To
its right is the home of Reeve J.C. Gill, and further
right, the home of architect G.D. Curtis.

The home of George's brother, T.S. Nye, who made his fortune from the sale of Boer War grant land. Queens Street and Lonsdale Avenue, circa 1909.

Chief Joe Capilano, circa 1906.

The Squamish Indians experienced new pressures with the flood of people attracted to North Vancouver. One of their villages was situated east of the mouth of Mosquito Creek and had been a traditional seasonal settlement for many years. By 1869, it had been designated as a reserve. French Oblate fathers established a Catholic mission at the village in the 1860s, and for a time the Indians lived in relative seclusion from the white world. The Squamish had found employment at Moodyville and, where necessary, adapted their lifestyle to an industrial age. After 1900, loggers, settlers, and business people became more active in the territory surrounding the reserve. Even the waterfront reserve land was eyed jealously by the newcomers.[10]

Chief Joe Capilano's experiences illustrate some of the boom era's effects upon native people. Sahpluk, as Chief Joe was known to the Indians, was born in 1859 and must have lived much of his life apart from white society. Working as a laborer once an adult, his dealings with whites no doubt increased. Chief Joe became concerned with white domination of land and resources. In 1906 he led a delegation of Indian leaders to London to confront King Edward VII, and also became active in native rights grievances along the coast. When he died in 1910, many of his people's traditional lifestyles had been altered by the twentieth century. The land surrounding the Indian villages was rapidly being settled.[11]

The Mission Reserve prior to 1909. In that year, twin spires and other additions visible today were made to St. Paul's Catholic Church.

Volunteer land-clearing party at Victoria Park, 1905.

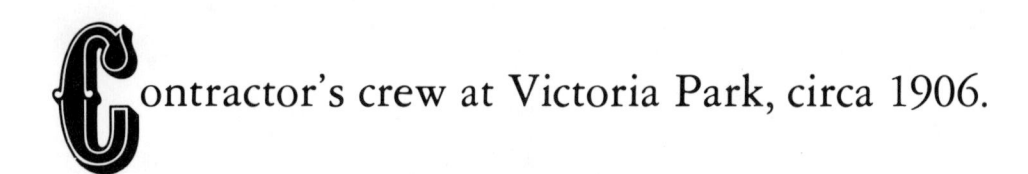

Contractor's crew at Victoria Park, circa 1906.

Nye's views of park landscaping and logging activity suggest that North Vancouverites viewed the land as a resource for public and private interests. It appears that all would agree the new city should have parks, but recreation and financial gain alike were motives for the setting aside of lands for this purpose. Victoria Park came into existence in 1905, when residents began clearing the stump-strewn land near Keith Road and Lonsdale Avenue. The job was completed by a contractor hired by the civic government. Property for this project had been donated by Colonel A. St. George Hammersley, of the Lonsdale Estate, and by the North Vancouver Land and Improvement Company. A similar scheme by the latter company was the creation in 1908 of the Grand Boulevard. The intention of this endeavor was to clear a wide parkland as the centerpiece in an exclusive residential district.

Meanwhile, much greater activity was afoot in the forests, where the lumber industry found bountiful cedar and fir. Extensive logging was vastly altering the appearance of some tracts on the North Shore. In response to the building boom, at least one lumber company expanded into real estate promotion, building and plumbing supply sales, and residential-commercial construction.[12]

Hauling scene showing the effects of logging upon the forest, circa 1906.

Nye supplied the images for this advertisement from *Henderson's Vancouver Directory 1910.*

North Vancouver's hotel business became a thriving enterprise prior to the Great War. Hotels were a favorite destination for Sunday excursionists from Vancouver, and also served as community centers for residents, especially during holidays. Swedish hotel entrepreneur Pete Larson was North Vancouver's best-known host. He constructed the Hotel North Vancouver in 1902 near the beach west of Lonsdale Avenue, and in 1909 his Canyon View Hotel opened for business near the edge of scenic Second Canyon, Capilano River. Only one of his rivals, the Palace, survives today, renamed the Olympic. No one would have imagined in 1909 that a prohibition measure, enacted during a world war eight years down the road, would deliver a crippling blow to hotel business throughout the province. Larson's hotels were no exception.

The Hotel North Vancouver was situated on Esplanade Street near Chesterfield Avenue. This view was taken about 1907 and was published as a color post card.

HOTEL NORTH VANCOUVER

Larson's Canyon View Hotel on the Capilano River boasted thirty rooms when completed in May, 1909.

The Palace Hotel, Second Street East, circa 1907.

Second Canyon, Capilano River, circa 1909. A shingle-bolt flume designed to carry lengths of cedar is visible on the left side of the canyon. This entire scene was obliterated in the 1950s when the Cleveland Dam was built between the cliff apexes.

The Capilano River Valley attracted both hiker and timber entrepreneur in the century's first decade. As today, walkers, anglers, and picnickers sought the natural beauty of the river's canyons and forests. However, business enterprise saw fortunes to be made from the valley's timbered slopes. One outfit completed a most unusual venture in 1905. Typical of the almost limitless optimism of the time, but doomed to failure, the Burrard Inlet Flume and Boom Company constructed a wooden, nine-mile-long flume to carry shingle-bolts to the Inlet from the Capilano Valley. Although it was never a commercial success, the flume's catwalk provided the adventuresome with a breath-taking walk through Second Canyon, high above the rapids. The flume was also a challenge to small boys who attempted to ride cedar bolts as they floated down the length of the trough.[13]

Capilano River scene, circa 1908. Two men barely visible on the right bank give a sense of scale to this view.

CAPILANO RIVER NORTH VANCOUVER B.C.

Lynn Valley Road, circa 1906.

"Is the Lynn Valley all settled up? Not by any means; though at the present rate of influx, it will not be long before it is."[14] So warned one promoter in 1907. Although this booster's prediction was premature, the penetration of roads and the promise of street railway extension stimulated speculation and settlement. Logging was Lynn Valley's original reason for being, but during the building boom the valley's natural advantages and available land prompted residential growth. When the City of North Vancouver broke away, the District was left without an administrative and commercial center of its own. Lynn Creek, as the valley's settlement was known, became the District's nucleus after 1907. Some pioneers felt that the boom had infused life into the valley at the expense of a community spirit born out of a remote logging village past.[15]

Lynn Valley Road North Vancouver B.C.

Twin Falls, Lynn Creek, circa 1906.

LYNN CANYON, NORTH VANCOUVER, BC

The Sunset Club served Lynn Valley as a hotel. Circa 1907.

The summit, Grouse Mountain, circa 1907.

North Vancouver hikers on Grouse Mountain, 1906. G.G. Nye is standing at the bottom right.

The residents of the North Shore took time out from their work to explore their natural surroundings. They had access to a recreational environment as fine as any in the province with respect to fishing, hunting, hiking, and climbing. Trails and peaks that could challenge any level of ability were to be found in the range of mountains above the community. Vancouver-based mountaineering groups took the ferry across Burrard Inlet to enjoy these diverse opportunities, patronizing hotels and refreshment businesses enroute. For parties from North Vancouver, the summit of Grouse Mountain was a favorite day hike. Several chalet and scenic railway schemes were proposed for the summit, but none passed the promotion stage. As a result, the mountain and adjacent peaks remained unspoiled areas where the young could spend their leisure hours prior to the disruption of the Great War.

TOP OF GROUSE MTN.
1906

Lynn Valley Road, circa 1909.

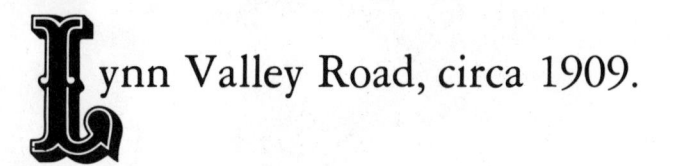

The boom years were to be short-lived. Suddenly, North Vancouver's bubble burst. Outside forces shattered the climate of prosperity and tranquillity experienced within the community. In 1913, the bottom dropped out of the real estate market and financial depression followed. Soon, all attention was focused on the First World War. Like other communities, North Vancouver's fortunes were unalterably tied to those of the nation; hence local residents continued to feel the force of economic and social undulations which swept Canada in the succeeding turbulent years.

The North Shore was prosperous again by the mid-1920s, but the great depression of the 1930s caused years of hardship. During the early '30s, the City and District governments found themselves incapable of providing necessary relief to citizens because tax money was not forthcoming. The rights which had accompanied incorporation, achieved

with great pride by the city fathers during the boom years, were revoked. Both City and District had no choice but to submit to government by a single commissioner.

Demand for ships by the allied forces during the Second World War lifted North Vancouver out of financial collapse by bringing the shipbuilding industry to its waterfront. Unprecedented suburban growth followed the war and the stereotype of North Vancouver as a "bedroom community" was strengthened. In recent years, new subdivisions and concentrations of apartment buildings have altered the settled landscape's appearance considerably.

In spite of these and other post-1900 changes, the "boom years" which George Nye captured in his photographs were perhaps the most dramatic in North Vancouver's history: a time when a confident, modern city rose on the forested North Shore.

Notes

1. Advertisement, *Prize List, Fifth Annual Exhibition* (North Vancouver Horticultural Association and Farmers' Institute, 1908), back cover.

2. Robert C. Brown and Ramsay Cook, *Canada 1896-1921: A Nation Transformed,* pp. 1-6.

3. *Fifth Census of Canada 1911,* p. 537, and Kathleen M. Woodward-Reynolds, "A History of the City and District of North Vancouver," p. vi, table G.

4. Alan Anderson and Betty Tomlinson, *Greetings From Canada: An Album of Unique Canadian Postcards from the Edwardian Era 1900-1916,* p. xiii.

5. Interviews with Molly Nye, North Vancouver, 1976-1977.

6. North Vancouver *Express,* 28 June 1907.

7. Kathleen Woodward-Reynolds, "A History," pp. 48-70.

8. Letter of identification, 1 July 1937, by William J. Irwin, accompanying photograph #1863. North Shore Archives, North Vancouver, B.C.

9. North Vancouver *Express,* 16 July 1909.

10. Harold Kalman, *Exploring Vancouver: Ten Tours of the City and its Buildings,* p. 218, and Woodward-Reynolds, "A History," p. 161.

11. James W. Morton, *Capilano: The Story of A River,* pp. 25-37.

12. Woodward-Reynolds, "A History," p. 122.

13. Morton, *Capilano,* p. 77.

14. North Vancouver *Express,* 28 June 1907.

15. Woodward-Reynolds, "A History," p. 91.

Bibliography

Anderson, Alan A., and Betty Tomlinson. *Greetings from Canada: An Album of Unique Canadian Postcards from the Edwardian Era 1900-1916.* Toronto: Macmillan of Canada, 1978.

Brown, Robert C., and Ramsay Cook. *Canada 1896-1921: A Nation Transformed.* Toronto: McClelland and Stewart, 1974.

Fifth Census of Canada 1911. Ottawa: 1912.

Henderson's Vancouver Directories 1905-1910. Henderson Publishing Company.

Hopkins, J. Castell. *The Canadian Annual Review of Public Affairs 1905-1913.* Toronto: The Annual Review Publishing Company.

Kalman, Harold. *Exploring Vancouver: Ten Tours of the City and its Buildings.* Vancouver: University of British Columbia Press, 1974.

Morton, James W. *Capilano: The Story of a River.* Toronto: McClelland and Stewart, 1970.

North Vancouver *Express,* 1906-1910.

Ormsby, Margaret A. *British Columbia: A History.* Vancouver: MacMillan, 1958.

Woodward-Reynolds, Kathleen M. "A History of the City and District of North Vancouver." Master's thesis, University of British Columbia, 1943.

Don Bourdon is an Archivist at the Glenbow-Alberta Institute in Calgary. Previously, he worked for the City of Vancouver Archives and for the North Shore Museum and Archives. Mr. Bourdon serves as a volunteer for the latter organization.

PRESS-GANGED!

The London press-gang rounding up men for the fleet in 1790. 'Pressing' was seen as unjust but a necessary evil in wartime. However, only seamen were liable to impressment. Others who were swept up and could prove they were not seamen were generally released.

CAT O'NINE TAILS

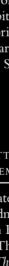

'The cat' symbolizes the harshness of naval life in Nelson's time. But it is often forgotten that life ashore could be much worse and that, to operate safely and effectively, sailing warships required unique skills and teamwork. Punishment played only a small part compared to mutual trust and good organisation.

NELSON'S KING

George III came to the throne in 1760, aged 22, and his 60-year reign saw Britain become the world's dominant seafaring power. Despite Nelson's part in this, his public and private behaviour meant the King rarely approved of him. Portrait by Sir William Beechey.

THE BATTLE OF QUIBERON BAY, 20 NOVEMBER 1759

The greatest naval victory of the Seven Years War, when Admiral Hawke routed the French fleet off southern Britanny, foiling plans for an invasion of Britain. This painting by Richard Paton shows the French *Thesée* sinking.

THE YOUNG NELSON

oratio Nelson was born at Burnham Thorpe, Norfolk, on 29 September 1758, the third of five sons in a family of eight. His mother, whom he remembered with great affection, died when he was nine and he was educated at Norwich Grammar School and at North Walsham. Though small, he was from the first a spirited and determined dare-devil.

NELSON AS A BOY

This miniature, by an unknown artist, is believed to show Nelson at the age of eight.

NELSON'S MOTHER

Catherine Suckling (1725-67) was the daughter of a Prebendary of Westminster and related to the influential Walpole family. A woman of strong character, this portrait shows her at the age of 18.

THE PARSONAGE HOUSE, BURNHAM THORPE

Nelson's birthplace was originally two big cottages with garden and glebe farm attached. Nelson also lived here with his wife while on half pay in the 1790s. The imagined group in the garden includes him as a boy with his parents. The house was demolished in 1802.

THE NELSON FAMILY BIBLE

Nelson had a very devout upbringing and remained deeply religious all his life. At the age of 17, while unwell at sea as a midshipman, he had a strange vision of 'a golden orb' which confirmed his trust in divine providence and determined him quite consciously to 'be a hero... and brave every danger'. Thereafter he was practically fearless for his own fate.

THE REVEREND EDMUND NELSON

Nelson's father (1722–1802) was a gentle, pious, strict and rather impractical man. His letters to his son are formal but affectionate and he developed a close relationship with Nelson's wife, Fanny. She persuaded Sir William Beechey to come and paint this portrait of him in 1800.

MIDSHIPMAN NELSON

*N*elson joined the 64-gun *Raisonnable* at Chatham in March 1771, aged 12, following an offer from his uncle, Captain Suckling to start one of Edmund's sons on a naval career in his own ship. After early but inactive service, Suckling sent him to the West Indies in a merchantman to widen his experience. He then joined an Arctic expedition, after which he went to India in the frigate *Seahorse*, before he returned to pass his lieutenant's examination in London in 1777.

CAPTAIN THE HON. CONSTANTINE PHIPPS

Later Lord Mulgrave, he led Nelson's 1773 Arctic voyage in command of the *Racehorse* and formed a good opinion of the young midshipman. A portrait by Ozias Humphrey.

NELSON AND THE BEAR

One night Nelson and a companion left the *Carcass* without permission, to shoot a polar bear. Nelson's gun misfired and only a crack in the ice prevented the bear killing him before a cannon shot from the *Carcass* scared it away. To Captain Lutwidge's demand for an explanation, Nelson said he wanted the bear skin as a present for his father. From a painting by Richard Westall.

MIDSHIPMEN READING

A very rare image of 'young gentlemen' studying in the gunroom of the frigate *Pallas* in 1737, drawn by one of her lieutenants. But for the date and ship, Nelson could be one of these boys.

'UNCLE MAURICE'

Captain Maurice Suckling (1725-78) the brother of Nelson's mother, was a distinguished officer who rose to be Comptroller of the Navy. When told Nelson wanted to join the Navy he wrote: 'What has poor Horace done, who is so weak, that he...should be sent to rough it out at sea', but his early help was a great advantage to his nephew.

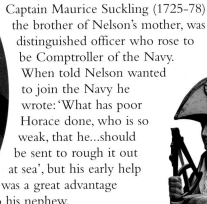

MIDSHIPMAN'S DIRK 1775

'Mids' carried these long dirks rather than swords. This one, 16in (40.5cm) overall, was sold by Banks of Plymouth Dock, now Devonport.

'THE LITTLE MIDSHIPMAN'

This carved wooden figure is the sign for an instrument seller's shop. It in fact shows a lieutenant in 1787 full-dress uniform, with his octant.

IN THE ARCTIC

In 1773 Nelson joined the *Carcass*, bomb vessel, one of two ships sent to seek a passage through the Arctic. Both were nearly trapped in the ice.

EVENTS OF NELSON'S LIFE

~1772 JULY~
Returns to *Triumph*, at the Nore

~1773 APRIL-OCTOBER~
Arctic expedition in *Carcass*

~NOVEMBER~
To India in *Seahorse*

~1773 DECEMBER~
'Boston Tea Party'; growing rebellion in American colonies

~1774~
Louis XVI becomes king of France

~1775~
American War begins: actions at Lexington, Concord and Bunker Hill

~1776 4 JULY~
American rebels declare independence at Philadelphia

~1776 SEPTEMBER~
Returns home sick. Joins *Worcester* on convoy duty

THE WEST INDIES

*N*elson's next years were spent largely in frigates, first in the *Lowestoffe* to the West Indies. He rose rapidly and in 1779 was appointed captain of the *Hinchinbroke*. In 1780 he returned home to recover from fever caught on a land operation in Central America. He then commanded the frigate *Albemarle* in the North Sea, to America and in the Caribbean. After a brief stay in France he returned to the West Indies in 1784 in the frigate *Boreas*.

CAPTAIN HORATIO NELSON, 1781

Painted for Captain Locker, by John Francis Rigaud, this was begun when Nelson was a lieutenant in 1779 and finished in 1781 when he was a captain.

CAPTAIN WILLIAM LOCKER (1731–1800)

Nelson's captain in the *Lowestoffe*, who became his friend and mentor. Nelson later wrote: 'I have been your scholar...It is you who taught me to to board a Frenchman'.

NELSON AND COLLINGWOOD

Nelson (*left*) met Cuthbert Collingwood (*right*) when both were lieutenants in the West Indies. They remained lifelong friends, Collingwood being second-in-command at Trafalgar. These are pictures they did of each other in 1785.

NELSON BOARDING A PRIZE

When the *Lowestoffe* captured an American prize in November 1777 the sea was so rough the first lieutenant would not try boarding it. Nelson as second lieutenant did so. Richard Westall's picture shows him bidding farewell to Captain Locker as he leaves the *Lowestoffe*.

LOWESTOFFE, 32 GUNS, BUILT 1761

A fine original model of the frigate in which Nelson first served as a lieutenant under Captain Locker. Frigates had only a single deck of guns and were used as convoy escorts and scouts for the fleet. No admiral ever had enough of them.

SEEKING LOVE & FAVOUR

In 1782 at New York, Nelson met Prince William Henry, third son of George III and a naval midshipman. He later served under Nelson in the West Indies as a junior captain when, to curry royal patronage, Nelson rashly supported him in a number of minor blunders. This, and Nelson's high-handed suppression of illegal trade between British merchants in the Caribbean and the newly independent United States, made him unpopular both there and with the Admiralty in England.

PRINCE WILLIAM HENRY

Shown here as a midshipman with Admiral Digby, the Prince became Duke of Clarence and, in 1830, the 'Sailor King' William IV. He and Nelson continued to correspond to Nelson's death, after which he wrote: 'I did not think it possible but for one of my dearest relations, to have felt what I have done, and what I still do, for poor Nelson'.

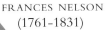

Nelson commanded the 28-gun *Boreas* from 1784 to 1787. This drawing by Nicholas Pocock shows her off the Dutch West Indian island of St Eustatius, with a French frigate in the distance.

ADMIRAL LORD HOOD

Hood first commanded Nelson at New York in 1782 but coolled towards him after Nelson made himself unpopular for his zeal over the Navigation Acts. When war with France broke out in 1793 however, Hood, now a Lord of Admiralty, backed Nelson's appointment to the 64-gun *Agamemnon*.

FRANCES NELSON
(1761–1831)

'Fanny' Nisbet was the widow of a doctor, with a small son, and keeping house for her wealthy uncle on the island of Nevis when Nelson met her in 1784.

EVENTS OF NELSON'S LIFE

~1782 NOVEMBER~
Joins Admiral Lord Hood at New York

~1783 MARCH~
His attack on Turk's Island, West Indies, fails

~JULY~
Returns to England

~SEPTEMBER~
End of American War. Pitt the Younger, prime minister (–1801 and 1804–06)

~1784 MARCH~
Captain of *Boreas*, to West Indies. Attempts to enforce Navigation Acts

~1787 MARCH~
Marries Frances Nisbet on Nevis

~DECEMBER~
Boreas pays off in England. Spends five years at Burnham Thorpe

~1789~
French Revolution begins

COLONIAL TRADE

A chart decoration, showing merchants and hogsheads of tobacco on a quay in Maryland. After 1783, direct trade between the now independent Americans and the British West Indian colonies was illegal. But it was also lucrative and tolerated, and Nelson's attempts to stop it made him enemies everywhere.

LIMERICK LACE OVERSKIRT OF FANNY'S WEDDING DRESS

In 1787, Nelson married Fanny on Nevis and, on return to England, they spent five years together at Burnham Thorpe until war broke out again in 1793, when their lives slowly became more separate. Fanny's anxiousness and inefficiency irritated Nelson, who needed practical arrangements at home and craved admiration.

REVOLUTIONARY WAR

*I*n 1788 Louis XVI summoned the French Parliament, which had not met since 1614. Within a year, the resulting drive for political reform triggered the French Revolution. Republican extremists seized power and in January 1793 a 'Reign of Terror' began with the execution of King Louis. In February, France declared war on Britain, Austria and Prussia.

RICHARD PARKER

In 1797 the British fleet mutinied for better conditions, first at Spithead (Portsmouth) and then at the Nore (Sheerness). Parker, shown here as a French Revolutionary, was among those hanged as leaders of the Nore mutiny.

VICTORY LEAVING THE CHANNEL

Seen flying Lord Hood's flag, outward bound with the fleet, including Nelson's *Agamemnon*, to support French Royalists at Toulon in 1793.

MADAME GUILLOTINE

The guillotine was introduced in Revolutionary France in 1792, as an egalitarian and humane means of execution. This 63lb (28.4kg) blade and sliding block is from one captured in the French West Indies in 1794.

BATTLE OF THE GLORIOUS FIRST OF JUNE, 1794

Lord Howe's Channel Fleet's victory over the French Brest Squadron, 300 miles west of Ushant (Brittany), was the first major naval action of the war.

'SAILORS, THE REPUBLIC OR DEATH'

A flag from the boarding division of the French *L'Amérique*, one of the ships captured by Lord Howe at the Glorious First of June, 1794.

'CONSEQUENCES OF A SUCCESSFUL FRENCH INVASION'

Detail from a print of 1810 by James Gillray, showing the French - by then no longer republicans but citizens of Napoleon's empire - setting up a guillotine in the old House of Lords, Westminster.

MORTELLA TOWER

The good anchorage in San Fiorenzo Bay, north Corsica, was guarded by an ancient watchtower on Mortella (myrtle) Point, with a heavy gun on top which fired red-hot shot. When attacked by Royal Naval ships in 1794 it put up such stiff resistance that it became the model for Britain's Martello Towers, built on the south coast from 1805.

NELSON'S WRITING

Nelson's regular and unexceptional right-hand script was quickly replaced after he lost that arm in 1797 by the spiky left-hand scrawl which is one of the most distinctive hand-writings of famous people.

NELSON'S SHIPS

An imaginary grouping at Spithead, showing his principal vessels from 1793. *Agamemnon*, 64 guns, is on the extreme left with *Vanguard*, 74, his Nile flagship broadside on and *Elephant*, 74, his temporary flagship at Copenhagen in front. In the distance is the *Captain*, 74, which he commanded as a commodore at Cape St Vincent and on the right *Victory*, 100 guns, his Trafalgar flagship. The picture is by Nicholas Pocock.

WAR IN THE MEDITERRANEAN

While Hood's fleet besieged Toulon, Nelson in the *Agamemnon* patrolled the western Mediterranean, saw action against French frigates and in 1794 lost the sight of his right eye during the taking of Corsica. In July 1795 he distinguished himself in the capture of the French 80-gun *Ça Ira* and in 1796 he was appointed Commodore. By the end of the year, however, the British left the Mediterranean for strategic reasons.

CAPE ST. VINCENT & TENERIFE

On 14 February 1797 the Spanish fleet attempted to sail from Cartagena to Cadiz. The British, now under Admiral Jervis, inflicted a severe defeat on them off Cape St. Vincent, with Nelson the hero of the hour. In July, Nelson (now Sir Horatio and a Rear-Admiral) led a risky attack on Spanish ships at Santa Cruz in the Canary Islands. It ended with retreat and the loss of his right arm.

'NELSON'S PATENT BRIDGE FOR BOARDING FIRST-RATES'

At Cape St. Vincent, Nelson in the 74-gun *Captain* almost single-handedly blocked the retreat of part of the Spanish force. This daring attack ended with his capture of the Spanish *San Nicolas*, 80 guns, and from her the 114-gun *San Josef*, as shown in the painting by Sir William Allan.

BELL OF THE *SAN JOSEF*

The *San Josef* was built of mahogany in Cuba, then a Spanish colony. After Nelson captured her she was taken into the Royal Navy.

NELSON BOARDS THE *SAN JOSEF*

With the *San Nicolas* entangled with the *San Josef*, Nelson ordered the charge to take her too. From a painting by George Jones.

NAVAL MEDAL

In 1794 the first modern naval medals were awarded to the admirals and senior captains at the Battle of the Glorious First of June. The same pattern was awarded for other actions, including Cape St. Vincent.

JOHN JERVIS, EARL OF ST. VINCENT (1735-1823)

Nelson's formidable superior commanded the Mediterranean and Channel Fleets and was First Lord of the Admiralty, 1801-05. He thought highly of Nelson as a fighter but came to disapprove of his political judgement and private life. By Sir William Beechey.

NELSON WOUNDED AT TENERIFE

While landing to seize Spanish ships in the harbour, Nelson's right arm was shattered above the elbow by a musket ball and was amputated that night. A painting by Richard Westall.

THE HERO OF THE NILE

*I*n spring 1798, disturbing reports suggested that Napoleon was gathering forces at Toulon to attack Egypt and, beyond that, British interests in India. Nelson, now recovered from his wound, was sent to reconnoitre but missed the sailing of Napoleon's task-force in May, a few days before his flagship *Vanguard* was dismasted by a gale. With more ships from Jervis, he then spent the next two months searching the eastern Mediterranean for Napoleon's fleet. On the evening of 1 August 1798 he found and almost totally destroyed it in Aboukir Bay, near Alexandria, in the most crushing victory of his career.

NAPOLEONIC FURY

James Gillray's image of Napoleon swearing to extirpate the English after the Battle of the Nile, which trapped his army in Egypt until their defeat there in 1801.

THE BATTLE BEGINS

Nicholas Pocock's painting shows the French at anchor. Nelson's fleet is outflanking the head of their line, between the first ship and the Aboukir Fort, to attack on their unprepared side in what became largely a night action.

NILE FREEDOM BOX

This gold and enamel box was given to Nelson's flag-captain at the Nile, Edward Berry, with the Freedom of the City of London. It shows the battle with the French flagship *L'Orient* exploding.

LIGHTNING CONDUCTOR

From the mainmast of the French flagship, *L'Orient*, of Admiral Brueys. Nelson kept this as a souvenir of the Nile. The coffin in which he was buried was also made from the same mast.

TRIBUTES OF VICTORY

The musket and canteen were among the Sultan of Turkey's gifts to Nelson after the Nile. The silver cup by Paul Storr was presented to him by London's Turkey Merchants.

CAPTAIN THOMAS FOLEY

Foley's *Goliath* led the outflanking manoeuvre which began the Battle of the Nile and was the key to its success. He was able to do this in shoal waters by having the most up-to-date local charts - ironically, French ones.

NELSON THE HERO

The most famous of Lemuel Abbott's portraits of him, painted after the Battle of the Nile from a sketch of 1797. It shows him wearing the diamond *chelengk* in his hat, awarded him by the Sultan of Turkey.

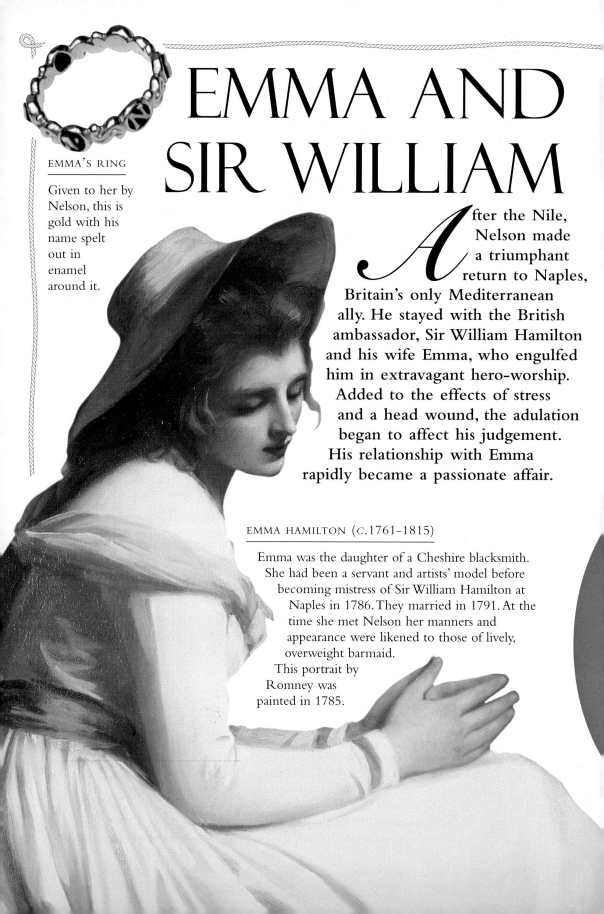

EMMA AND SIR WILLIAM

EMMA'S RING

Given to her by Nelson, this is gold with his name spelt out in enamel around it.

After the Nile, Nelson made a triumphant return to Naples, Britain's only Mediterranean ally. He stayed with the British ambassador, Sir William Hamilton and his wife Emma, who engulfed him in extravagant hero-worship. Added to the effects of stress and a head wound, the adulation began to affect his judgement. His relationship with Emma rapidly became a passionate affair.

EMMA HAMILTON (C.1761–1815)

Emma was the daughter of a Cheshire blacksmith. She had been a servant and artists' model before becoming mistress of Sir William Hamilton at Naples in 1786. They married in 1791. At the time she met Nelson her manners and appearance were likened to those of lively, overweight barmaid.

This portrait by Romney was painted in 1785.

GIFTS TO EMMA

A bloodstone brooch of Nelson which she wore, a gold toothpick case which Nelson gave her at Christmas 1804 and a gold and enamel snuff box inscribed 'Dear Emma from NB'. The miniature, by John Dunn, shows Emma as she was when Nelson met her in the 1790s.

EVENTS OF NELSON'S LIFE

~1801 JANUARY~
Promoted Vice-Admiral of the Blue under Lord St. Vincent in Channel Fleet. Separates from wife. To Emma, a daughter, Horatia

~FEBRUARY~
In *St George*, joins fleet for Baltic under Admiral Hyde Parker

DRESS FLOUNCE

From a dress worn by Emma at a fete in Palermo, 1799. It has 'Nelson' and 'Brontë' (his Neapolitan ducal title) embroidered under swags of oak leaves.

SIR WILLIAM HAMILTON (1730-1803)

Hamilton was British envoy at Naples, 1764-1800. He pioneered the study of volcanoes and was a great collector of Classical vases. Much older than Emma, his second wife, he never acknowledged her true relationship with their mutual friend, Nelson.

'THE HERO OF THE NILE'

Nelson's vain but exhausted appearance after the Nile, weighed down with the sword and scarlet cloak given him by the Sultan of Turkey. By James Gillray.

NAPLES

Nelson was made Duke of Brontë in Sicily by King Ferdinand for his part in suppressing the Neapolitan revolt. This insignia of the Neapolitan Order of St. Ferdinand, and of Merit is the only one of his medals to survive. The rest were stolen from the Royal Naval College, Greenwich, in 1900.

Naples - 'the Kingdom of the Two Sicilies'- comprised Sicily and most of Italy south of Rome, ruled over by the despotic and dissolute King Ferdinand IV.

Late in 1798, when the French invaded Neapolitan territory, Nelson evacuated the royal family to Palermo. After a Royalist counter-attack, a truce with the French made by Ferdinand's war minister was cancelled by Nelson and the short-lived 'Vesuvian Republic' collapsed amid savage Royalist reprisals. These were condoned by Nelson who also had the turncoat head of the Neapolitan navy ruthlessly hanged at his own yardarm.

REAR-ADMIRAL NELSON, 1799

This shows Nelson's exhausted appearance after the Nile and how he wore his hat to keep it clear of the forehead wound he received there. Painted at Naples by Leonardo Guzzardi.

FIDEI ET MERITO

ADMIRAL LORD KEITH

As new Mediterranean commander-in-chief he censured Nelson for his refusal to leave Naples when ordered, and strongly disapproved of his behaviour with the Hamiltons.

THE FLEET IN THE BAY OF NAPLES

An unusual view by an Italian artist, showing Nelson's squadron when it called at Naples while searching for Napoleon's fleet before the Battle of the Nile.

EVENTS OF NELSON'S LIFE

~1801 2 APRIL~
Battle of Copenhagen (in *Elephant*). Relieves Parker as Baltic commander in May. Created Viscount Nelson

~JULY~
Commands defence flotilla in South East England. Abortive attack on Boulogne invasion flotilla

~1802 MARCH~
Peace af Amiens signed

QUEEN MARIA-CAROLINA

Queen of Naples and sister of the executed French queen, Marie-Antoinette. She was talkative, pious, astute and practically ran Naples for her husband. Emma became her friend and confidante.

KING FERDINAND IV

He was mainly interested in hunting and women, and left government largely to his wife and half-English prime minister.

COPENHAGEN

After returning to England with the Hamiltons in 1800, Nelson was sent to the Baltic under Admiral Parker, to break a hostile alliance of Denmark, Russia, Prussia and Sweden. Neutralising the Danish fleet was the first task, achieved by Nelson with a detached force which Parker gave him. This bombarded the Danes anchored off Copenhagen until a truce was agreed. Nelson was rewarded with a viscountcy.

'I REALLY DO NOT SEE THE SIGNAL'

The hat Nelson wore at the Battle of Copenhagen and beneath which he raised his telescope to his blind eye, refusing to see Admiral Parker's signal to withdraw. The seal is the one with which he signed the offer of truce 'To the Brothers of Englishmen, the Danes'.

A DANISH TROPHY

This small brass gun was one of those taken at Copenhagen, though now on an English cast iron carriage. The opposing Danish force consisted of unrigged ships operating as floating batteries, with two heavily armed offshore forts.

'DIDO IN DESPAIR'

Gillray shows the now fat Lady Hamilton lamenting Nelson's departure for the Baltic, while on the other side of the bed Sir William Hamilton sleeps on. The title refers to the desertion of Dido, Queen of Carthage, by her lover Aeneas.

THE BATTLE OF COPENHAGEN

Nelson's line of 74-gun ships, anchored abreast of the Danes off Copenhagen on 2 April 1801.

THE MAD TSAR

Paul I of Russia, the mentally unstable Tsar, was a prime architect of the 'Armed Neutrality' of the northern powers against Britain. His murder nine days before the Battle of Copenhagen ensured its collapse.

EVENTS OF NELSON'S LIFE

~1802~
Settles at Merton with the Hamiltons

~1803 APRIL~
Sir William Hamilton dies

~MAY~
Napoleonic War starts (–1815)

MERTON

*W*hen Nelson returned overland to England with the Hamiltons in 1800, Emma was already pregnant with his daughter Horatia, born in late January 1801. He abandoned his wife, despite her pleas for a reconciliation, and with Emma's help purchased Merton Place, a modest country house in what is now south-west London. When in England he, Emma and Sir William continued to live here together, to the scandal of respectable society. It was from Merton that he left for Trafalgar and his death in 1805.

HORATIA, AGED TEN

Nelson's daughter later married a clergyman and died aged 80, never knowing who her mother was, though she did realise Nelson was her father.

NILEUS

Among the various pets at Merton was a dog called Nileus, which in fact ran away not long after joining the household. This is his silver collar.

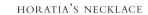

HORATIA'S NECKLACE

A gift to her from Nelson. On another occasion she asked him for a dog and he sent her a gold one as part of a necklace decoration.

FROM NELSON'S HAND

One of his left-hand kid gloves with his name written in the cuff by Emma; his visiting card and the combined knife and fork he used after loss of his right arm.

Viscount Nelson, Duke of Bronte

EVENTS OF NELSON'S LIFE

~1803 JULY~
Joins *Victory* off Toulon as Commander-in-Chief in Mediterranean. Blockades French until early 1804

~1804 APRIL~
Promoted Vice-Admiral of the White

~MAY~
Napoleon proclaimed Emperor of France

~1805 MARCH-MAY~
French Toulon fleet and Spaniards from Cadiz escape to West Indies. Nelson pursues

~JUNE~
Combined Fleet resail for Europe, fight inconclusive action off Cape Finisterre with Calder's British squadron, 22 July, and enter Cadiz

CUP AND PLATE

A large quantity of Nelson's china survives. This plate and cup are from a Coalport service, the plate carrying his full coat of arms.

TRAFALGAR

*I*n 1805 Napoleon ordered that Admiral Villeneuve's combined Franco-Spanish fleet make a diversionary expedition to the West Indies, before returning to cover an invasion of England. Nelson chased them there and back, to Cadiz, and the invasion plan was abandoned. The enemy fleet then sailed to support French forces in the Mediterranean and, on 21 October 1805, was defeated by Nelson off Cape Trafalgar.

Combined French & Spanish Fleet

British Fleet

'THE NELSON TOUCH'

Nelson's tactic was to attack in two lines, cutting off and overwhelming the enemy centre and rear before their vanguard could turn and assist.

TELESCOPE

Used at Trafalgar by John Pasco, *Victory's* signal lieutenant, who hoisted Nelson's famous signal; 'England expects that every man will do his duty'.

THE BATTLE OF TRAFALGAR

J.M.W. Turner's painting of 1824 is a Romantic interpretation of events rather than a record of them. It shows *Victory*, with the word 'duty' spelt out by the flags on her mainmast, and the captured French *Redoutable* sinking under her bows.

'KISS ME HARDY'

Shortly after 1.00pm Nelson was shot by a sniper and died about 4.30pm in *Victory's* cockpit. A.W. Devis's painting of his death shows Captain Hardy (standing) and the Rev. Dr Scott, Nelson's chaplain, rubbing his breast to relieve the pain. Walter Burke, the purser, supports the pillow and Nelson's valet, Guitan, looks at Dr Beatty who feels for the pulse.

NELSON'S PIGTAIL

'Pray let dear Lady Hamilton have my hair...', said the dying admiral. It was cut off after his death and is still tied in this queue at the back.

EVENTS OF NELSON'S LIFE

~1805 JULY~
Nelson reaches Gibraltar

~AUGUST~
Returns to England

~SEPTEMBER~
In *Victory* with fleet off Cadiz

~19 OCTOBER~
Combined Fleet leave Cadiz

~21 OCTOBER~
Battle of Trafalgar. Death of Nelson

~5 DECEMBER~
Victory, with Nelson's body, arrives home

FUNERAL

Nelson's body was returned to England in *Victory*, preserved in a cask of brandy. After lying in state in the Painted Hall of Greenwich Hospital, it was taken up-river on 8 January 1806 to the Admiralty in Whitehall. On the 9th, amid vast crowds and with the Prince of Wales leading the mourners, a huge procession bore it to burial in St Paul's Cathedral. Lady Hamilton's end was less glorious. Grief-stricken but ever-extravagant, she was imprisoned for debt in 1813. On release she retired to Calais, where, drinking heavily, she died in 1815.

IN MOURNING

John Salter, Nelson's jeweller, made 58 mourning rings for family and close friends attending the funeral. Some open to reveal a lock of his hair, though the example here is in a small brooch.

FUNERAL TICKET

Separate tickets were issued for the funeral procession and the service. This is the portrait painter John Hoppner's for the procession.

THE COFFIN

Nelson's body was enclosed in four coffins, the inner one made from *L'Orient*'s mainmast. This miniature was made on the *Victory* for her purser, Walter Burke.

SPANISH ENSIGN

This 50 x 32 ft (15.25 x 8.9m) ensign is from the Spanish *San Ildefonso*, captured at Trafalgar.

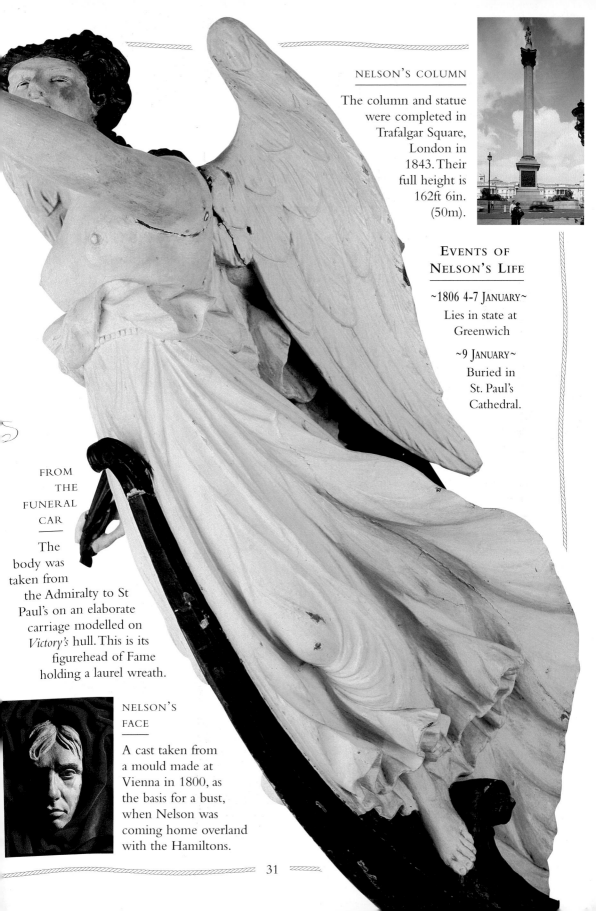

NELSON'S COLUMN

The column and statue were completed in Trafalgar Square, London in 1843. Their full height is 162ft 6in. (50m).

EVENTS OF NELSON'S LIFE

~1806 4-7 JANUARY~
Lies in state at Greenwich

~9 JANUARY~
Buried in St. Paul's Cathedral.

FROM THE FUNERAL CAR

The body was taken from the Admiralty to St Paul's on an elaborate carriage modelled on *Victory's* hull. This is its figurehead of Fame holding a laurel wreath.

NELSON'S FACE

A cast taken from a mould made at Vienna in 1800, as the basis for a bust, when Nelson was coming home overland with the Hamiltons.

DID YOU KNOW ?

Nelson's height - Nelson is often shown as small compared to others. Though slender, he was in fact about 5ft 6in (168cm), not short for his day.

'I have only one eye - I have a right to be blind sometimes. I really do not see the signal'. (At Copenhagen, 1801). Nelson is often said to have lost his right eye and is shown with a patch over it. In fact he only lost its useful *sight* and even this may have improved at the end of his life when he was more worried about the strain on his *left*. Over this he wore a shade on his hat to reduce glare.

Nelson's Trafalgar signal - Nelson wanted to hoist 'England *confides* that every man will do his duty' but *Victory's* signal lieutenant, John Pasco, asked to use 'expects', which needed fewer flags. 'That will do', said Nelson, 'Make it directly'. His last signal was, 'Engage the enemy more closely'.

Nelson's last words - These were very carefully recorded. He did say 'Kiss me, Hardy' to his old friend and flag-captain. Hardy did so and then knelt again and repeated the gesture in farewell. He was not present when Nelson died, the admiral's last coherent words being 'Thank God I have done my duty'.

Nelson's body - Nelson's body was put in one of *Victory's* largest water casks, a 159-gallon leaguer, filled with brandy. This was topped up with 'spirits of wine' at Gibraltar before leaving for England. Dr Beatty later took out the fatal musket ball and, on his death in 1842, it was given to Queen Victoria.

Nelson's hero - The hero Nelson most admired was Major-General James Wolfe, who was killed aged 32 during his victorious attack on Quebec in 1759. Nelson asked Sir Benjamin West, who painted a famous picture of Wolfe's death, to record his own similarly should he be killed. West did so in 1806-07; it is now in Liverpool.

Admirals' ranks - Until 1864, admirals, vice-admirals and rear-admirals each had three levels of seniority according to 'squadronal colours' - red, white and blue. A captain, on promotion to 'flag-rank' became a Rear-Admiral of the Blue, then White, then Red before moving up to Vice-Admiral of the Blue. Nelson died as a Vice-Admiral of the White. The naval toast 'a bloody war or a sickly season' refers to the fact that, once a man had reached 'post' rank - (i.e. captain) promotion into 'dead mens' shoes' was automatic, even though continued active employment was not.

Ships of the line - Those considered large enough to lie in the line of battle and fight an opponent of similar size broadside to broadside. By Nelson's time the smallest was the 64-gun two-decker, such as the *Agamemnon,* and the largest the 100-gun three-decker, like *Victory.* Of all these the most useful all-rounder was the 74-gun ship, also a two-decker. Over half the fleet at Trafalgar was 74s.

ACKNOWLEDGEMENTS

Ticktock would like to thank: Liz Rowe, Graham Rich and Tracey Pennington for their assistance.
Photography by Tina Chambers and Peter Robinson, National Maritime Museum.
Printed in Hong Kong.

Nelson was published in association with the National Maritime Museum, Greenwich.
Copyright © 2006 ticktock Entertainment Ltd
Text copyright © National Maritime Museum

We are grateful to the National Maritime Museum, Greenwich for permission to reproduce their copyright photographs for *Nelson,* with the exception of the following: page 31 Nelson's Column - C.O.I. Copies of the National Maritime Museum's photographs can be obtained from their Customer Services Section.

A CIP Catalogue for this book is available from the British Library. ISBN 1 86007 507 X